First published in Great Britain in 1996 by Brockhampton Press, a member of the
Hodder Headline Group, 20 Bloomsbury Street, London WC1B 3QA.

This series of little gift books was made by Frances Banfield, Kate Brown, Laurel Clark,
Penny Clarke, Clive Collins, Melanie Cumming, Nick Diggory, Deborah Gill, David
Goodman, Douglas Hall, Maureen Hill, Nick Hutchison, John Hybert, Kate Hybert,
Douglas Ingram, Simon London, Patrick McCreeth, Morse Modaberi, Tara Neill, Anne
Newman, Grant Oliver, Michelle Rogers, Nigel Soper, Karen Sullivan and Nick Wells.

Compilation and selection copyright © 1996 Brockhampton Press.

ISBN 1 86019 438 9

A copy of the CIP data is available from the British Library upon request.

Produced for Brockhampton Press by Flame Tree Publishing,
a part of The Foundry Creative Media Company Limited,
The Long House, Antrobus Road, Chiswick W4 5HY.

Printed and bound in Italy by L.E.G.O. Spa.

THE LITTLE BOOK
OF
Golf

Selected by Beth Hurley

Golf is definitely a four-letter word.
But which — love, or hate?

Anonymous

Golf is the most fun you can have
without taking your clothes off.

Chi Chi Rodriguez

That does look like very good exercise.
But what is the little white ball for?

Ulysses S. Grant

Golf is essentially an exercise in masochism
conducted out of doors.

Paul O'Neil

Golf is so popular simply because it is the best game in
the world at which to be bad.

A. A. Milne

Jack Nicklaus ... The route to immortality lies by way of wins in major championships and Nicklaus's closest rival in some golfing Valhalla is Bobby Jones.

The Who's Who of Golf

Golf is not a funeral, though both can be very sad affairs.

Bernard Darwin

GOLFER: 'This is a terrible course. I've never played on a worse one.'
CADDIE: 'But this isn't the course! We left that an hour ago.'

Ian Woosnam ... on his anonymity and lack of inches: 'Perhaps if I dyed my hair peroxide blond and called myself the great white tadpole that would help?'

Old golfers never die — they simply lose their drive.

Golf is a lot of walking broken up
by disappointment and bad arithmetic.

Nick Faldo ... 'He has developed
the best swing since Tarzan.'
Colin M. Farman

If you watch a game, it's fun.
If you play it, it's recreation.
If you work at it, it's golf.
Bob Hope

Why waste good shots in practice
when you might need them in a match?
W. C. Hagen

It's good sportsmanship to not pick up lost golf balls
while they are still rolling.
Mark Twain

Winning is the only thing that matters.

Jack Nicklaus

Golf is not a game of good shots,
it is a game of bad shots.

Ben Hogan

The only shots you can be dead sure of are
those you've had already.

Alexander Revell

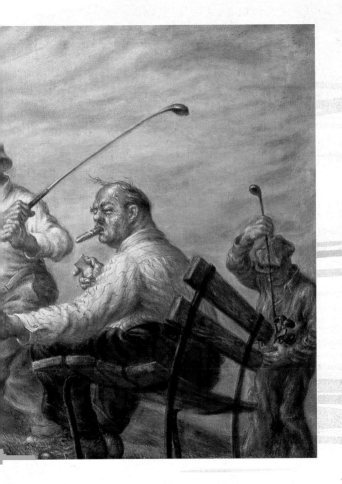

45.—THE ELEGANCIES
OF GOLF.

If you drink, don't drive.
Don't even putt.

Dean Martin

I find it more satisfying to be a bad player at golf.
The worse you play, the better you remember
the occasional good shot.

Nubar Gulbenkian

It is impossible to imagine Goethe or Beethoven
being good at billiards or golf.

H. L. Mencken

Golf is not just exercise; it is an adventure, a romance ...

Harold Segall

.... humiliations are the essence of the game.

Alistair Cooke

The friends you make on the golf course
are the friends you make for life.

J. A. Valentine

It's almost impossible to remember how tragic a place
the world is when one is playing golf.

Robert Lynd

The game was easy for me as a kid,
and I had to play a while to find out how hard it is.

Raymond Floyd

If there is any larceny in a man,
golf will bring it out.

Paul Gallico

The way you are on the golf course
is usually the way you are in life.

Tammie Green

Golf has none of the essentials of a great game.
It destroys rather than builds up character, and tends
to selfishness and ill-temper.

B. J. T. Bosanquet

Does not a caddy in truth take charge of our lives
and control all our thoughts and actions
while we are in his august company?

Baron Moynihan

I'd like to see the fairways more narrow. Then everyone
would have to play from the rough, not just me.

Seve Ballesteros

There are three ways of learning golf: by study,
which is the most wearisome, by imitation which is the
most fallacious, and by experience,
which is the most bitter.

Robert Browning

I'd rather have him as a partner than an opponent ...
That's because he can be pretty sneaky.
He'll get out there on the first tee and try to make a
match. The first thing he does is
talk his opponents out of their handicaps.

Bing Crosby about Bob Hope

An *alter kocker* is a man who can no longer
do something that he once could ...
There are certain activities that are recognizable
for old people that only an *alter kocker* gets
involved in and golf is one.

Jackie Mason, *How To Talk Jewish*

I know I'm getting better at golf because
I'm hitting fewer spectators.

Gerald R. Ford

I have a tip that can take five strokes
off anyone's golf game. It's called an eraser.

Arnold Palmer

Golf is a game in which the ball lies poorly
and the players well.

Art Rosenbaum

Golf is like fishing and hunting. What counts is the
companionship and fellowship of friends,
not what you catch or shoot.

George Archer

For me, it's a game to be played with fresh air in your
lungs and joy in your heart.

Peter Alliss, *More Bedside Golf*

Playing golf with any President is handy. If you hit a ball into the rough and it stops near a tree, the tree becomes a Secret Service man and moves away.

Bob Hope, *Thanks for the Memory*

I did not want to turn to playing golf, because golf is about as much exercise as shuffling cards.

Bill Cosby, *Time Flies*

Sometimes it's difficult for spectators to know where to stand at all, with any guarantee of safety.

Peter Alliss, *More Bedside Golf*

If you go out with a man who plays golf,
your biggest problem will be not to laugh the first time
you see him in action. Once they get on the course,
the most sober, steadfast and demure individuals
suddenly blossom out like court jesters,
in the most brilliant colours and fashions —
lemon-yellow caps, pale blue anoraks,
cherry-pink trousers. And when they wiggle their feet
to get their stance right they look exactly like
cats preparing to pee.

Jilly Cooper, *Men and Super Men*

CRUDEN BAY

BAY

BY · EAST · COAST · ROUTE
FULL INFORMATION FROM ANY
L · N · E · R AGENCY

President Ford was playing golf with ice hockey star Gordie Howe. At the twelfth hole, Howe conceded a two-foot putt to his distinguished opponent. Ford insisted on taking the shot — and missed. 'We won't count that one,' said Howe. Pointing to the reporters and Secret Service men at the edge of the green, Ford said, 'Maybe you won't, but they will.'

Gobble: a putt made with undue force.

The City Golf Club in London is unique among such organizations in not possessing a golf course, ball, tee, caddy or bag. Its whole premises just off Fleet Street do not contain a single photograph of anything that approaches a golfing topic ...

Stephen Pile, *The Least Successful Golf Club*

If you think it's hard to meet new people, try picking up the wrong golf ball.

Jack Lemmon

Most people play a fair game of golf –
if you watch them.

Joey Adams

Particularly pleasing is the story of Queen Alexandra
muddling golf with croquet and, when on the green,
gaily hitting her husband's golf-ball away from the hole
and then pushing her own in.

Arthur Marshall, *Sunny Side Up*

There is no truth in the idea that the person who hits
the most balls will become the best golfer. Golf is a
bizarre sport. You can work for years and years on your
game without making any improvement in your score.

Fred Couples

Mildred Didrikson was a champion golfer, an Olympic
gold medalist, an all-American basketball player,
a nifty billiards player and holder of a
world record for throwing a baseball (296 feet).

Donald Steel, *The Guinness Book of Golf Facts and Feats*

Grass: in a bunker on a golf course,
grass is not usually considered as a hazard.

I like the thought of playing for money instead of
silverware. I never did like to polish.

Patty Sheehan

If your opponent is playing several shots in vain
attempts to extricate himself from a bunker, do not
stand near him and audibly count strokes.
It would be justifiable homicide if he wound up his
pitiable exhibition by applying his niblic to your head.

Harry Vardon

I've known the agony and the ecstasy.
I'm convinced I've got more of both ahead of me.

Greg Norman

Faldo's got more nerve than me. I couldn't do what he
does. Golfers are visible to everyone,
their job is harder than mine.

Nigel Mansell

When Nicklaus plays well, he wins,
when he plays badly, he comes second.
When he plays terrible, he's third.

Johnny Miller

I never hit a shot even in practice without having a
very sharp, in-focus picture of it in my head. It's like a
colour movie. First I 'see' the ball where I want to
finish. Then the scene quickly changes and I 'see' the
ball going there. Then there's a sort of fade-out, and the
next scene shows me making the kind of swing that will
turn the previous images into reality.

Jack Nicklaus

The par here at Sunningdale is 70 and anything under
that will mean a score in the sixties.

Stevie Rider

Ice, Snow: on the golf course, ice and snow are not
considered to be hazards.

The golfer ... is never old until he is decrepit. So long as Providence allows him the use of two legs active enough to carry him round the green, and two arms supple enough to take a 'half swing', there is no reason why his enjoyment in the game need be seriously diminished.

Arthur Balfour

The game of golf was invented by the devil.

Winston Churchill

Ernie J. Gill

GOLF de la Soukra TUNIS

Fitness counts for less in golf than in any other game,
luck enters into every minute of the contest,
and all play is purely incidental to,
and conditioned by, gamesmanship.

Stephen Potter, *The Complete Upmanship*

Golf is a good walk spoiled.

Mark Twain

The most exquisitely satisfying act in the world of golf is
that of throwing a club. The full backswing,
the delayed wrist action, the flowing follow-through,
followed by that unique whirring sound,
reminiscent only of a passing flock of starlings, are
without parallel in sport.

Henry Longhurst

A day spent in a round of strenuous idleness.

William Wordsworth

The highest golf course in the world is the
Tuckbu golf club in Morococha, Peru,
which is 4,369 metres [14,335 feet] above sea-level.
The lowest golf course in the world is Furnace Creek,
Death Valley, California which is 67 metres
[220 feet] below sea level.
On the moon the energy expended on a
mundane 300 yard drive would achieve, craters
permitting, a distance of 1 mile.

Donald Steel, *The Guinness Book of Golf Facts and Feats*

All I've got against golf is that it takes you so far
from the club house.

Eric Linklater, *Poet's Pub*

Edward Ray ... The features of Ray's game that were
most remarkable were his long hitting, violent recovery
play ... but he is said to have never relinquished the
pipe between his teeth.

The Who's Who of Golf

46.—ALEX. HERD.

Playing the game I have learned the meaning of
humility. It has given me an understanding of the
futility of human effort.

Abba Eban

Mole hill: on the golf course,
a mole hill is considered to be a loose impediment.

At the Benson and Hedges tournament, Fulford, York,
1981, Bernard Langer's second shot to the 17th
in the round finished up a tree.
Undeterred, he climbed the tree and
hit his ball from the tree.

Donald Steel, *The Guinness Book of Golf Facts and Feats*

Years ago we discovered the exact point, the dead
centre of middle age. It occurs when you are too young
to take up golf and too old to rush up to the net.

Franklin P. Adams, *Nods and Becks*

'Daddy,' said the bright child, accompanying her father on a round of golf, 'why mustn't the ball go in the hole?'

Greg Norman ...
Norman soon won a reputation for savage hitting ...
in the 1979 Australian Open, he had a $100-a-hole side bet with Fuzzy Zoeller on the longest drive and came through easily.
The Who's Who of Golf

When you are playing well, you can hit the ball within a foot of where you want it to land.
Greg Norman

NORMAN WILKINSON

If it wasn't for golf, I don't know what I'd be doing.
If my IQ had been two points lower,
I'd have been a plant somewhere.

Lee Trevino

I never exaggerate. I just remember big.

Chi Chi Rodriguez

Mary Catherine Wright ... Always at the fore when the
question of great women players of all time is raised.
She began to play at the age of 11, encouraged by her
father, who had wanted a boy and had already
introduced her to baseball at the age of four.

The Who's Who of Golf

Some players today play two or three tournaments, get
tired, and then take a couple of weeks off. I couldn't
wait to get to the next tournament. If they're tired they
should go to bed early.

Ben Hogan

Golf is not relaxation, golf is everything, golf is a
philosophy, it's a religion, absolutely,
I mean really absolutely.

Sir Bob Reid

In a competition at Peace Haven, Sussex,
England in 1890, A. J. Lewis had 156 putts on one
green without holing out.

Donald Steel, *The Guinness Book of Golf Facts and Feats*

GOLFER: 'I've never played this badly before.'
CADDIE: 'You've played before?'

The difference between a sand bunker and water is the
difference between a car crash and an airplane crash.
You have a chance of recovering from a car crash.

Bobby Jones

The longer you play, the better chance
the better player has of winning.

Jack Nicklaus

Destiny plays a big part in everyone's life.
You play golf, you play good, you hit a good drive at
the last hole and it is in a divot hole in the middle of
the fairway. That has to be destiny.

Seve Ballesteros

GOLFER: 'Well Caddie, how do you like my game?'
CADDIE: 'It's terrific sir. Mind you I still prefer golf.'

Golf liars have one advantage over fishing liars –
they don't have to show anything to prove it.
Anonymous

CHIPPING SODBURY ...
Two huge drainage dykes cut through the course and
form a distinctive hazard on eleven holes.

BALLY BUNION ...
The Atlantic waves crash into the shore and no golfer
will ever feel closer to nature as he hunts his ball and
flights it through cross winds and breathtaking views.

GLOUCESTERSHIRE ...
The 12th is a drive straight up a hill, nicknamed
'Coronary Hill'.

YELVERTON ...
The fairways are tight but there is plenty of room.
The A. A. Guide to Golf Courses

Just about the greatest thing a man can do who doesn't
play golf for a living. That includes getting kissed by a
cheerleader, having cash money in your pocket,
owning a faithful dog, and anything
that has to do with marriage.

Lewis Grizzard, on shooting his first par game

For the golfer, Nature loses her significance. Larks, the
casts of worms, the buzzing of bees, and even children
are hateful to him ... Winds cease to be east, south,
west or north. They are ahead, behind or sideways,
and the sky is bright or dark, according
to the state of the game.

Sir W.G. Simpson, *The Art of Golf*

It's not whether you win or lose –
but whether I win or lose.

Sandy Lyle

33.—MacFoozle.
Chief of the Clan.

TONY JACKLIN ...
On winning Royal Lytham and St Anne's 1969 ...
In the last tee, it looked as if a bogie would see him
home. But Jacklin finished in style; he split the fairway
with the longest drive seen there all week.

The Who's Who of Golf

Nothing handicaps you as much in golf as honesty.

Anonymous

Golf's predictable structure is both comforting and
relaxing. We can almost predict the exact words our
playing partners will use to set up the game on the first
tee. This predictability provides a safe harbour for a few
hours to avoid some of the storms of the everyday
world. Golf absorbs our minds, and the mental
tribulations of our lives are put on hold
as we wrestle with errant drives,
pulled approach shots and missed putts.

Dr Richard H. Coop

NOTES ON ILLUSTRATIONS

Page 5 *The Tee-Off*, by Peter Szumowski (Private Collection). Courtesy of The Bridgeman Art Library; **Page 8-9** *Four Men, Golfer in Red Jumper*. Courtesy of Hobbs Golf Collection, Northumberland; **Page 11** *Golf at the Belfry*, by Judy Joel (Private Collection). Courtesy of The Bridgeman Art Library; **Page 12-13** *Aspects of Urban Life: Golf*, by Paul Cadmus (National Museum of America Art, Smithsonian). Courtesy of The Bridgeman Art Library; **Page 14** Detail from *'Cope's Golfers'*, Edwardian Cigarette Cards in an Album (Private Collection). Courtesy of The Bridgeman Art Library; **Page 16** *Bass Rock, North Berwick*. Courtesy of Hobbs Golf Collection, Northumberland; **Page 18** *Golf in Italy*, book cover illustration, by Max Minon (Private Collection). Courtesy of The Bridgeman Art Library; **Page 20-1** *Colfing at Westward Ho!*, by Francis Powell Hopkins (Private Collection). Courtesy of The Bridgeman Art Library; **Page 23** *Holed in One*, by Louis Wain (Victoria & Albert Museum, London). Courtesy of The Bridgeman Art Library; **Page 24** *Study of Colfers for Kipling's Almanack of Twelve Sports*, by William Nicholson (Private Collection). Courtesy of The Bridgeman Art Library; **Page 26-7** *Cruden Bay, 1900+*. Courtesy of Hobbs Golf Collection, Northumberland; **Page 29** *Portrait of the Golfer, Tom Morris*, by James McIntosh Patrick (Private Collection). Courtesy of The Bridgeman Art Library; **Page 30** *A Tour in Italy – Roman Campagna with Golfers*, by Edina Vittorio Accornero (Private Collection). Courtesy of The Bridgeman Art Library; **Page 33** *Silloth on the Solway*. Courtesy of Hobbs Golf Collection, Northumberland; **Page 34** *Chicago Tribune Cover, June 11, 1922, Portrait of a Woman Golfer*, by Maude Martin Ellis (Private Collection). Courtesy of The Bridgeman Art Library; **Page 36-7** *Take Cover*, by Ernest J. Gill (Private Collection). Courtesy of The Bridgeman Art Library; **Page 38-9** *North Berwick*. Courtesy of Hobbs Golf Collection, Northumberland; **Page 40** *Golf de la Soukra, Tunis*. Courtesy of Hobbs Golf Collection, Northumberland; **Page 43** Detail from *'Cope's Golfers'*, Edwardian Cigarette Cards in an Album (Private Collection). Courtesy of The Bridgeman Art Library; **Page 45** *'Summer Troubles in the Tropics – Snake Casts on the Sahara Golf Course'* (Chris Beetles Ltd, London). Courtesy of The Bridgeman Art Library; **Page 46-7** *St Andrews*. Courtesy of Hobbs Golf Collection, Northumberland; **Page 47-8** *The Tee-Off*, by Peter Szumowski (Private Collection). Courtesy of The Bridgeman Art Library; **Page 50-1** *Gleneagles Hotel, Perthshire*. Courtesy of Hobbs Golf Collection, Northumberland; **Page 53** *McCanny Late for Tee*, by Lawson Wood (Chris Beetles/Christopher Wood, London). Courtesy of The Bridgeman Art Library; **Page 54-5** *Oil Study for Frontispiece of R. Clark's 'Golf – A Royal & Ancient Game'* (Private Collection). Courtesy of The Bridgeman Art Library; **Page 59** *The Tee-Off*, by Peter Szumowski (Private Collection). Courtesy of The Bridgeman Art Library.

Acknowledgements: The Publishers wish to thank everyone who gave permission to reproduce the quotes in this book. Every effort has been made to contact the copyright holders, but in the event that an oversight has occurred, the publishers would be delighted to rectify any omissions in future editions of this book. *Bedside Golf* and *More Bedside Golf*, Peter Alliss, reprinted courtesy of Fontana, a division of HarperCollins Publishers Ltd; *A Golfer's Companion*, eds Chris Plumridge and John Hopkins; *The Art of Coarse Golf*, Michael Green, published by Hutchinson, reprinted courtesy of Richard Scott Simon Agency; *Golf Shorts*, Clen Liebman, reprinted courtesy of Robson Books; *Time Flies*, Bill Cosby, reprinted courtesy of Bantam Press; *The Guinness Book of Golf Facts and Feats*, Donald Steel, reprinted courtesy of Guinness Publishing Limited; *The Art of Golf*, by Sir W.C. Simpson, as quoted in *Golf Forever, Work Whenever*, compiled by Michael Ryan © The Great Quotations Publishing Company; *Just Say a Few Words*, Bob Monkhouse, Lennard Books, Random House UK Ltd.